GETTING TO KNOW THE WORLD'S GREATEST ARTISTS

HENRI DE TOULOUSE-LAUTREC

WRITTEN AND ILLUSTRATED BY MIKE VENEZIA

CONSULTANT MEG MOSS

CHILDRENS PRESS®
CHICAGO

Cover: *At the Moulin Rouge: The Dance,* by Henri de Toulouse-Lautrec.
1890. Oil on canvas, 45 1/2 x 59 inches. Philadelphia Museum of Art,
The Henry P. McIlhenny Collection in memory of Frances P. McIlhenny.

Project Editor: Shari Joffe
Design: PCI Design Group, San Antonio, Texas
Photo Research: Jan Izzo

Library of Congress Cataloging–in–Publication Data

Venezia, Mike.
    Henry de Toulouse-Lautrec / written and illustrated by Mike Venezia.
    p.   cm. -- (Getting to know the world's greatest artists)
    ISBN 0-516-42283-9
    1. Toulouse-Lautrec, Henry de, 1864-1901--Juvenile literature.
    2. Artists--France--Biography--Juvenile literature.
    [1. Toulouse-Lautrec, Henry de, 1864-1901. 2. Artists.
    3. Painting, French. 4. Art Appreciation.] I. Toulouse-Lautrec, Henry de, 1864-1901.
    II. Title.   III. Series: Venezia, Mike. Getting to know the world's
    greatest artists.
    N6853. T6V44 1994
    760' .092--dc20
    [B]   94-36348
                                    CIP
                                    AC

18 19 20 R 10 09 08

Portrait of Toulouse-Lautrec at Villeneuve-Sur-Yonne, by Edouard Vuillard. 1898. Oil on cardboard, 15.35 x 11.81 inches. Musée Toulouse-Lautrec, Albi, France.

Henri de Toulouse-Lautrec was born in Albi, France, in 1864. Even though he came from one of the wealthiest families in Europe, Henri preferred to live among and paint pictures of everyday people who usually didn't have much money at all.

At the Moulin Rouge: The Dance, by Henri de Toulouse-Lautrec. 1890.
Oil on canvas, 45 $\frac{1}{2}$ x 59 inches. Philadelphia Museum of Art,
The Henry P. McIlhenny Collection in memory of Frances P. McIlhenny.

Henri de Toulouse-Lautrec is
best known for the lively scenes
he painted of theaters, dance halls,
and circuses in the exciting city of
Paris, France.

He found the dancers, singers, and circus people much more interesting to paint than the wealthy people he was used to seeing while he was growing up.

Divan Japonais, by Henri de Toulouse-Lautrec. 1893. Crayon, brush, spatter and transferred color lithograph, 30 $\frac{15}{16}$ x 23 $\frac{7}{16}$ inches. San Diego Museum of Art, Gift of the Baldwin M. Baldwin Foundation.

Henri de Toulouse-Lautrec was also known for the posters he made to advertise the dance halls and entertainers he enjoyed so much.

Many people think Henri's posters are his greatest works of art. Henri made them easy to read, and his large, flat areas of color got people's attention right away. The techniques he discovered are still used in posters and advertising art today.

Henri always seemed to be interested in art. When he was very young, he especially loved to draw horses, dogs, and other animals that lived on the farms that were part of his family's many large estates.

Henri even filled his school notebooks
with drawings.

When Henri was thirteen years old,
a terrible thing happened to him.
While he was getting up from a chair,
he tripped and broke his left leg.

It took months to heal. Just after it got better, Henri fell again and broke his right leg! No one was sure at the time, but today, most doctors agree that Henri had a rare disease that caused his bones to break easily. Henri's legs stopped growing after his accidents, and he had to be very careful for the rest of his life.

While Henri's legs were healing,
he began to paint and draw more
than ever to help pass the time.

Henri's father was very disappointed that his son wouldn't be able to join him in all the things he enjoyed, like hunting and horseback riding. Henri was disappointed, too, but decided to keep his interest in outdoor activities alive by drawing and painting the things he loved. Henri was about sixteen when he painted his father, Count Alphonse, driving his coach with a team of powerful horses.

Count Alphonse de Toulouse-Lautrec Driving His Mail Coach in Nice,
by Henri de Toulouse-Lautrec. 1881. Oil on canvas, 15.16 x 20.07 inches.
Musée du Petit Palais, Paris. Photograph, Musées de la Ville de Paris.
© 1994 Artists Rights Society (ARS), NY/SPADEM, Paris.

Adele de Toulouse-Lautrec In the Drawing Room at Malrome, by Henri de Toulouse-Lautrec. 1887. Oil on canvas, 23.23 x 21.26 inches. Musée Toulouse-Lautrec, Albi, France.

Henri also painted pictures of his mother and the people who worked around his family's homes. Because of his great interest in drawing and painting, Henri's parents agreed to let him study art more seriously.

Henri began his studies in the city of Paris, France, when he was seventeen years old. He learned all he could in the studios of some of the best-known artists in Paris.

Even though Henri learned a lot in his classes, he couldn't wait to go off on his own and start painting the exciting people and places he saw in Paris.

Henri became friends with Vincent van Gogh, a very exciting person he met in his art class. Vincent would later become a famous artist, too. Henri made a portrait of his friend sitting at a cafe table. Some people think it is one of the best portraits of Vincent van Gogh ever made.

Portrait of Vincent van Gogh, by Henri de Toulouse-Lautrec. 1887. Pastel on cardboard, 21.26 x 17.72 inches. Van Gogh Museum, Amsterdam, The Netherlands. Collection Vincent van Gogh Foundation.

Henri was able to show Vincent's concentration and restless energy, and capture the way Vincent really was at that exact moment in time.

Being able to show people in simple, real moments of their lives was one of Henri's greatest talents. Most artists of Henri's time painted pictures of people posing in their best clothes with fancy decorations and furniture around them.

Madame Poupoule Dressing, by Henri de Toulouse-Lautrec. 1898.
Oil on wood, 23.94 x 19.53 inches. Musée Toulouse-Lautrec, Albi, France.

Henri thought you could tell much more about people by showing them doing everyday things, like combing their hair or enjoying themselves at a Paris nightclub.

For three years, Henri spent almost every night at his favorite nightclub and dance hall, the Moulin Rouge. He drew pictures of all the activity around him, and became friends with the singers and dancers there.

The owner of the Moulin Rouge liked Henri's art and asked him to create a poster to help advertise his club. In the first poster he ever made, Henri showed two famous dancers of the time.

Henri's posters were printed in large numbers off of a smooth, flat stone. Prints made this way are called *lithographs*.

Henri's posters of the Moulin Rouge were put up all over Paris and became very popular right away.

Moulin-Rouge, by Henri de Toulouse-Lautrec. 1891. Brush and spatter lithograph, 75.2 x 46.06 inches. Musée Toulouse-Lautrec, Albi, France.

Henri was an expert at drawing, and he knew the importance of making his posters simple and easy to read from a distance. To grab your attention, he sometimes cut people and objects off at the picture's edge in surprising ways.

The way an
artist places
the shapes and
people in a
work is called
composition.

Courtesan and Servant in the Night Rain,
by Kitagawa Utamaro. c. 1798. Woodblock print,
15.16 x 10.24 inches. The Art Institute of Chicago,
Gift of Mr. and Mrs. Gaylord Donnelley,
1968.158. Photograph © 1994 The Art Institute
of Chicago. All Rights Reserved.

Henri got some ideas for
his compositions from
Japanese prints and
from photography, a
new art form that was
becoming popular at
the time. Henri had
some fun experimenting
with photography, as
you can see in the
photograph above.

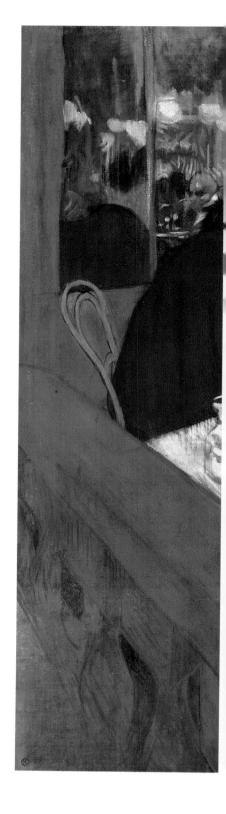

In one of his most famous paintings, Henri used a photographic composition idea by cutting off the lady's face at the edge of his picture. He also used strong, colorful, indoor lighting in a striking way. Henri included himself in this painting, too. He's the one walking across the room with his much taller cousin, Gabriel.

At the Moulin Rouge, by Henri de Toulouse-Lautrec. 1892-95. Oil on canvas, 48.43 x 55.51 inches. The Art Institute of Chicago, Helen Birch Bartlett Memorial Collection. Photograph © 1994 The Art Institute of Chicago. All Rights Reserved.

Henri was glad that his paintings and posters were getting attention, but deep down inside he always felt unhappy about being different from everyone else. To forget his problems, Henri began partying all night and drinking too much alcohol.

His parents and close friends began to worry about Henri's health and

At the Bar,
by Henri de
Toulouse-Lautrec.
1887. Oil on canvas,
21 3/4 x 16 1/2
inches. Virginia
Museum of Fine Arts,
Richmond, Collection
of Mr. and Mrs.
Paul Mellon.

the types of people he was
hanging around with. Henri
sometimes had to take long boat
trips to quiet places, where he
could rest and try to get better.

27

Marcelle Lender Dancing the Bolero in "Chilpéric", by Henri de Toulouse-Lautrec.
1895-96. Oil on canvas, 57 1/8 x 59 in. National Gallery of Art, Washington, D.C.
Gift (partial and promised) of Betsey Cushing Whitney in honor of John Hay Whitney,
for the 50th Anniversary of the National Gallery of Art. © 1994 National Gallery
of Art, Washington, DC. Photograph, Philip A. Charles.

Although Henri's health never really improved, he continued painting, drawing, and making prints of his favorite subjects.

The Jockey, by Henri de Toulouse-Lautrec. 1899. Color lithograph,
20 3/8 x 14 3/16 inches. National Gallery of Art, Washington, DC.,
Rosenwald Collection. © 1994 National Gallery of Art, Washington, D.C.
Photograph, Dean Beasom.

Henri de Toulouse-Lautrec died in 1901. Even though he was unhappy much of the time, Henri had lots of friends and a good sense of humor, and he was fun to be around.

Henri's friends included many famous artists whose work he admired, like Pierre-Auguste Renoir and Camille Pissarro.

Henri's favorite artist, though, was Edgar Degas.

Danseuse au Bouquet, by Edgar Degas.
Pastel over monotype, 15 7/8 x 19 7/8 inches.
Museum of Art, Rhode Island School of Design,
Gift of Mrs. Murray S. Danforth.

La Goulue at the Moulin Rouge, by Henri de Toulouse-Lautrec. 1891-92. Oil on cardboard, 31 1/4 x 23 1/4 inches. The Museum of Modern Art, New York, Gift of Mrs. David M. Levy. Photograph © 1995 The Museum of Modern Art, New York.

The scenes and people Henri painted and put in his posters were an important part of his everyday life.

Jane Avril Leaving the Moulin Rouge, by Henri de Toulouse-Lautrec. 1892. Essence on board, 33 1/4 x 25 inches. Wadsworth Atheneum, Hartford, Connecticut, Bequest of George A. Gay.

Henri de Toulouse-Lautrec had a very special talent for expressing people's moods and personalities. His paintings seem to let you in on a person's most private moments, both happy and sad.

If you get to see a real painting by Toulouse-Lautrec, you'll notice how he usually thinned his oil paints a lot. They sometimes look drippy, like watercolors. Henri drew with his brush

Detail of *In the Circus Fernando: The Ringmaster,* by Henri de Toulouse-Lautrec.

as much as he painted with it – he used his paintbrush almost like a pencil. Henri often painted on cardboard, too. He thought its natural brown color worked well as a background color.

The works of art in this book come from the museums listed below:
The Art Institute of Chicago, Chicago, Illinois
Musée du Petit Palais, Paris, France
Musée Toulouse-Lautrec, Albi, France
Museum of Art, Rhode Island School of Design, Providence, Rhode Island
The Museum of Modern Art, New York, New York
National Gallery of Art, Washington, D.C.
Philadelphia Museum of Art, Philadelphia, Pennsylvania
San Diego Museum of Art, San Diego, California
Van Gogh Museum, Amsterdam, The Netherlands
Virginia Museum of Fine Arts, Richmond, Virginia
Wadsworth Atheneum, Hartford, Connecticut